English Made Super Easy 1

English Made Super Easy 1
英语超级容易学1

JOSCELYN QUEK

PARTRIDGE

To order additional copies of this book, contact
Toll Free 800 101 2657 (Singapore)
Toll Free 1 800 81 7340 (Malaysia)
orders.singapore@partridgepublishing.com

www.partridgepublishing.com/singapore

目录

前言

我写这本书的目的，主要是要让学生们更容易、更快速、更有效地学习英语。

这本书适合小孩或成人初学者，可在自修自习时用，也可当作辅助教材。

主要的内容有词汇、语法要点、不同类型的英语句子和问题。宗旨是要让初学者熟悉简单的英语句子，然后尝试应用在日常生活中，无需顾虑太多的语法细节。

建议学生们先学 50 - 100 个词汇，然后再学习简单的句子和问题。

真心希望这本书能成为英语初学者不可缺少的良伴。

祝学习愉快！

1. 语法

1. 动词的时式　Verb Tenses

英文的动词有分现在式、过去式、
进行时式和未来式等。

例如：

I eat a pear everyday.
我每天吃一个梨。

I ate a pear yesterday.
我昨天吃了一个梨。

I have eaten a pear.
我已经吃了一个梨。

I am eating a pear now.
我现在在吃梨。

I shall eat a pear tomorrow.
我明天将会吃一个梨。

2. 单数动词和复数动词

Singular and Plural Verbs

例如：

I sing a song.
我唱一首歌。

He sings a song.
他唱一首歌。

She sings a song.
她唱一首歌。

We sing a song.
我们唱一首歌。

They sing a song
他们唱一首歌。

3. 单数名词和复数名词

Singular and Plural Nouns

例如：

1. a dog 一只狗

   many dogs 很多只狗

   a few dogs 几只狗

2. a cake 一个蛋糕

   many cakes 很多个蛋糕

   a few cakes 几个蛋糕

4. 英文没有量词

例如：

a dog 一只狗

a book 一本书

a chair 一张椅子

2. 简单的句子

a 一个

1. I draw a cup.
   我画一个杯。

2. I draw a bag.
   我画一个皮包。

3. I draw a pen.
   我画一支笔。

4. I draw a dog.
   我画一只狗。

5. I draw a chair.
   我画一张椅子。

6. I draw a door.
   我画一扇门。

an 一个

如果名词的第一个字母是 a, e, i, o, 或 u,
就要用an。

1. I draw an axe.
   我画一支斧头。

2. I draw an ant.
   我画一只蚂蚁。

3. I draw an eye.
   我画一只眼睛。

4. I draw an elephant.
   我画一只大象。

5. I draw an egg.
   我画一个鸡蛋。

6. I draw an ice cream.
   我画一支雪糕。

1. I draw an iron.
   我画一个熨斗。

2. I draw an ox.
   我画一只牛。

3. I draw an oven.
   我画一个电炉。

4. I draw an umbrella.
   我画一把雨伞。

5. I draw an animal.
   我画一只动物。

6. I draw an onion.
   我画一粒洋葱。

the　指定某个

1. I draw the airplane.
   我画那架飞机。

2. I draw the giraffe.
   我画那只长颈鹿。

3. I draw the doll.
   我画那个洋娃娃。

4. I draw the tree.
   我画那棵树。

5. I draw the flower.
   我画那朵花。

6. I draw the kangaroo.
   我画那只袋鼠。

没有指定 一个或某个

1. I draw houses.
   我画屋子。

2. I draw tigers.
   我画老虎。

3. I draw papayas.
   我画木瓜。

4. I draw bananas.
   我画香蕉。

5. I draw wind.
   我画风。

6. I draw water.
   我画水。

my　我的

1. My dog is sick.
   我的狗生病。

2. My face is round.
   我的脸是圆形的。

3. My bag is red.
   我的皮包是红色的。

4. My room is clean.
   我的房间很干净。

5. My hair is neat.
   我的头发很整齐。

6. My boss is generous.
   我的老板很慷慨。

give 给

1. I give you a plate.
   我给你一个盘。

2. I give you a bowl.
   我给你一个碗。

3. I give you a table.
   我给你一张桌子。

4. I give you a fork.
   我给你一支叉。

5. I give you a banana.
   我给你一条香蕉。

6. I give you a pot.
   我给你一个锅。

like　喜欢

1. I like the dog.
   我喜欢这只狗。

2. I like the movie.
   我喜欢这部电影。

3. I like the piano.
   我喜欢这架钢琴。

4. I like the fridge.
   我喜欢这个冰箱。

5. I like the restaurant.
   我喜欢这间餐馆。

6. I like the pattern.
   我喜欢这个款式。

1. I like to cook.
   我喜欢煮菜。

2. I like to exercise.
   我喜欢运动。

3. I like to dance.
   我喜欢跳舞。

4. I like to swim.
   我喜欢游泳。

5. I like to travel.
   我喜欢旅行。

6. I like to think.
   我喜欢思考。

1. I like to play games.
   我喜欢玩游戏。

2. I like to watch television.
   我喜欢看电视。

3. I like to buy shoes.
   我喜欢买鞋子。

4. I like to wear hats.
   我喜欢戴帽子。

5. I like to wear glasses.
   我喜欢戴眼镜。

6. I like to comb hair.
   我喜欢梳头发。

can 会 / 可以

1. I can make cakes.
   我会做蛋糕。

2. I can make bread.
   我会做面包。

3. I can dance.
   我会跳舞。

4. I can swim.
   我会游泳。

5. I can sing.
   我会唱歌。

6. I can drive.
   我会驾车。

want 要

1. I want to jump.
   我要跳。

2. I want to travel.
   我要去旅行。

3. I want to speak.
   我要讲话。

4. I want to listen.
   我要听。

5. I want to run.
   我要跑。

6. I want to walk.
   我要走。

1. I want to open the door.
   我要开门。

2. I want to write a letter.
   我要写一封信。

3. I want to sweep the floor.
   我要扫地。

4. I want to close the window.
   我要关窗。

5. I want to buy a watch.
   我要买一支手表。

6. I want to choose a colour.
   我要选一个颜色。

1. I want to go to the zoo.
   我要去动物园。

2. I want to go to the market.
   我要去菜市场。

3. I want to go to my office.
   我要去我的办公室。

4. I want to go to the supermarket.
   我要去超级市场。

5. I want to go to the shopping centre.
   我要去购物中心。

6. I want to go to America.
   我要去美国。

this 这

1. This is a ball.
这是一粒球。

2. This is a table.
这是一张桌子。

3. This is a knife.
这是一把刀。

4. This is a camera.
这是一个相机。

5. This is a doll.
这是一个洋娃娃。

6. This is a panda.
这是一只熊猫。

these   这些

1. These are umbrellas.
   这些是雨伞。

2. These are rings.
   这些是戒指。

3. These are watches.
   这些是手表。

4. These are candies.
   这些是糖果。

5. These are slippers.
   这些是拖鞋。

6. These are trucks.
   这些是货车。

that   那

1. That is a kite.
   那是一个风筝。

2. That is a tiger.
   那是一只老虎。

3. That is a lion.
   那是一只狮子。

4. That is an aeroplane.
   那是一架飞机。

5. That is a boat.
   那是一艘船。

6. That is a helicopter.
   那是一架直升机。

those   那些

1. Those are pencils.
   那些是铅笔。

2. Those are cherries.
   那些是樱桃。

3. Those are toys .
   那些是玩具。

4. Those are workers.
   那些是工人。

5. Those are students.
   那些是学生。

6. Those are cups.
   那些是杯子。

in 在

1. The pen is in the box.
   那支笔在盒子里。

2. The umbrella is in the bag.
   雨伞在皮包里。

3. I am in the car.
   我在车子里。

4. I am in the classroom.
   我在课室里。

5. I am in the toilet.
   我在厕所里。

6. The bird is in the cage.
   那只鸟在笼子里。

of   的

1. This is the name of my teacher.
   这是我老师的名字。

2. This is the story of lady Diana.
   这是戴安娜王妃的故事。

3. This is the answer of the question.
   这是这问题的答案。

4. This is the title of the book.
   这是那本书的书名。

5. This is the name of the restaurant.
   这是那间餐馆的名字。

6. This is the date of his birthday.
   这是他生日的日期。

near   靠近

1. I stay near my office.
   我住在我的办公室附近。

2. I sit near the window.
   我坐在窗边。

3. My house is near the river.
   我的屋子靠近那条河。

4. My school is near the cinema.
   我的学校靠近戏院。

5. The shop is near the library.
   那间店靠近图书馆。

6. My office is near the restaurant.
   我的办公室靠近那间餐馆。

verb tenses 动词的时式

1. I eat an apple everyday.
   我每天吃一个苹果。

2. I am eating an apple now.
   我现在在吃苹果。

3. I have eaten an apple.
   我已经吃了一个苹果。

4. I ate an apple yesterday.
   我昨天吃了一个苹果。

5. I was eating an apple just now.
   刚才我正在吃苹果。

6. I shall eat an apple tomorrow.
   明天我将吃一个苹果。

1. I wash my clothes everyday.
   我每天洗衣服。

2. I am washing my clothes now.
   我现在在洗衣服。

3. I have washed my clothes.
   我已经洗衣服了。

4. I washed my clothes yesterday.
   我昨天洗了衣服。

5. I was washing my clothes just now.
   刚才我正在洗衣服。

6. I shall wash my clothes tomorrow.
   明天我将洗衣服。

1. I dance everyday.
   我每天跳舞。

2. I am dancing now.
   我现在在跳舞。

3. I have danced.
   我已经跳了一支舞。

4. I danced yesterday.
   我昨天跳舞了。

5. I was dancing just now.
   刚才我正在跳舞。

6. I shall dance tomorrow.
   明天我将会跳舞。

1. I drink coffee everyday.
   我每天喝咖啡。

2. I am drinking coffee now.
   我现在在喝咖啡。

3. I have drunk a cup of coffee.
   我已经喝了一杯咖啡。

4. I drank a cup of coffee yesterday.
   我昨天喝了一杯咖啡。

5. I was drinking coffee just now.
   刚才我正在喝咖啡。

6. I shall drink coffee tomorrow.
   明天我将喝咖啡。

1. I clean the toilet everyday.
   我每天洗厕所。

2. I am cleaning the toilet now.
   我现在在洗厕所。

3. I have cleaned the toilet.
   我已经洗厕所了。

4. I cleaned the toilet yesterday.
   我昨天洗厕所了。

5. I was cleaning the toilet just now.
   刚才我正在洗厕所。

6. I shall clean the toilet tomorrow.
   明天我将会洗厕所。

before   之前

1. I ate an apple before noon.
我中午之前吃了一个苹果。

2. I came before 4 o'clock.
我四点之前来了。

3. I slept before eleven o'clock.
我十一点之前睡觉了。

4. I woke up before eight o'clock.
我八点之前起身了。

5. I brushed my teeth before ten o'clock.
我十点之前刷牙了。

6. He cried before the audience.
他在观众面前哭了。

am 是

1. I am a doctor.
   我是一名医生。

2. I have been a doctor for 5 years.
   我当医生已有五年了。

3. I was a doctor in the past.
   我以前是一名医生。

4. I had been a doctor before I went
   to China.
   去中国之前，我一直是一名医生。

5. I shall be a doctor.
   我将成为一名医生。

6. I shall be a carpenter.
   我将成为一名木匠。

1. I am a dentist.
   我是一名牙医。

2. I have been a dentist for 5 years.
   我当牙医已有五年了。

3. I was a dentist in the past.
   我以前是一名牙医。

4. I had been a dentist before I went to China.
   去中国之前，我一直是一名牙医。

5. I shall be a dentist.
   我将成为一名牙医。

6. I shall be a postman.
   我将成为一名邮差。

1. I am a hawker.
   我是一名小贩。

2. I have been a hawker for 5 years.
   我当小贩已有五年了。

3. I was a hawker in the past.
   我以前是一名小贩。

4. I had been a hawker before I went to China.
   去中国之前，我一直是一名小贩。

5. I shall be a hawker.
   我将成为一名小贩。

6. I shall be a waiter.
   我将成为一名侍应生。

1. I am a salesman.
   我是一名售货员。

2. I have been a salesman for 5 years.
   我当售货员已有五年了。

3. I was a salesman in the past.
   我以前是一名售货员。

4. I had been a salesman before I went to China.
   去中国之前，我一直是一名售货员。

5. I shall be a salesman.
   我将成为一名售货员。

6. I shall be a beautician.
   我将成为一名美容师。

1. I am an engineer.
   我是一名工程师。

2. I have been an engineer for 5 years.
   我当工程师已有五年了。

3. I was an engineer in the past.
   我以前是一名工程师。

4. I had been an engineer before I went to China.
   去中国之前，我一直是一名工程师。

5. I shall be an engineer.
   我将成为一名工程师。

6. I shall be a teacher.
   我将成为一名教师。

1. I am happy.
   我很开心。

2. I have been happy.
   我一直很开心。

3. I was happy yesterday.
   我昨天很开心。

4. I had been happy before I got married.
   结婚之前，我一直很开心。

5. I shall be happy.
   我将会很开心。

6. I shall be sad.
   我将会很伤心。

1. I am active.
   我很活跃。

2. I have been active.
   我一直很活跃。

3. I was active in the past.
   我以前很活跃。

4. I had been active before I got
   married.
   结婚之前，我一直很活跃。

5. I shall be active.
   我将会很活跃。

6. I shall be careful.
   我将会很小心。

1. I am lazy.
   我很懒惰。

2. I have been lazy.
   我一直很懒惰。

3. I was lazy yesterday.
   我昨天很懒惰。

4. I had been lazy before I got married.
   结婚之前，我一直很懒惰。

5. I shall be hardworking.
   我将会很勤劳。

6. I shall be busy.
   我将会很忙。

1. I am greedy.
   我很贪心。

2. I have been greedy.
   我一直很贪心。

3. I was greedy yesterday.
   我昨天很贪心。

4. I had been greedy before I got married.
   结婚之前，我一直很贪心。

5. I shall be greedy.
   我将会很贪心。

6. I shall be obedient.
   我将会很听话。

1. I am naughty.
   我很顽皮。

2. I have been naughty.
   我一直很顽皮。

3. I was naughty yesterday.
   我昨天很顽皮。

4. I had been naughty before I got married.
   结婚之前，我一直很顽皮。

5. I shall be naughty.
   我将会很顽皮。

6. I shall be nervous.
   我将会很紧张。

me 我

1. He scolded me.
他骂我。

2. He taught me.
他教我。

3. He hit me.
他打我。

4. He asked me.
他问我。

5. He praised me.
他称赞我。

6. He encouraged me.
他鼓励我。

on 上

1. I sit on the sofa.
   我坐在沙发上。

2. I write on the paper.
   我写在纸上。

3. I played tennis on Tuesday.
   我星期二打网球。

4. I came here on Friday.
   我星期五来这里。

5. My book is on the table.
   我的书在桌子上。

6. I sleep on the bed.
   我睡在床上。

to   至

1. I go to the library everyday.
   我每天去图书馆。

2. I went to the zoo yesterday.
   昨天我去动物园。

3. I went to the park yesterday.
   昨天我去公园。

4. I wrote a letter to him.
   我写了一封信给他。

5. I walked from my school to the cafe.
   我从我的学校走去咖啡馆。

6. I am listening to the music.
   我在听音乐。

at   介词

1. I am at the restaurant.
   我在餐馆。

2. I am at the shop.
   我在店里。

3. I wait for you at the park.
   我在公园等你。

4. I am at Scott Road.
   我在史各士路。

5. I look at him.
   我看着他。

6. I shouted at him.
   我对着他喊。

into　进入

1. I went into the house.
   我进了屋子。

2. I went into the room.
   我进了房间。

3. I look into the mirror.
   我看着镜子。

4. I fell into the cave.
   我跌进了山洞里。

5. I look into his eyes.
   我看着他的眼睛。

6. I came into her life.
   我走进了她的生活。

from 从

1. I am from Singapore.
   我来自新加坡。

2. I am from China.
   我来自中国。

3. I came here from my office.
   我从办公室来这里。

4. I came here from the airport.
   我从机场来这里。

5. I borrowed a book from the library.
   我从图书馆借了一本书。

6. I came back from work.
   我放工回来。

for 介词

1. I bought a toy for him.
   我买了一个玩具给他。

2. I bought a sofa for him.
   我买了一套沙发给他。

3. I closed the window for him.
   我帮他关了窗。

4. I prepared breakfast for him.
   我帮他准备了早餐。

5. I washed the clothes for him.
   我帮他洗了衣服。

6. I care for him.
   我关心他。

with 和

1. I went with my mother.
我和我的妈妈去。

2. I sang with my sister.
我和姐姐一起唱。

3. I went to the park with him.
我和他去公园。

4. I went to the mall with him.
我和他去购物中心。

5. I quarrelled with my husband.
我和我的丈夫吵架。

6. I discussed with my colleague.
我和我的同事讨论。

up   上

1. I climbed up the hill.
   我爬上山。

2. I went up the stairs.
   我爬上楼梯。

3. I climbed up the tree.
   我爬上树。

4. I picked up a wallet.
   我捡起了一个钱包。

5. I lifted up a box.
   我抬起了一个箱子。

6. I picked up a leaf.
   我捡起了一片叶子。

down 下

1. I walked down the hill.
   我走下山坡。

2. I walked down the staircase.
   我走下楼梯。

3. I fell down the stairs.
   我跌下楼梯。

4. I put down the knife.
   我放下刀子。

5. I looked down from the top.
   我从高处往下看。

6. I put down my suitcase.
   我放下皮箱。

under 之下

1. I slept under a tree.
   我睡在一棵树下。

2. I hid under the bed.
   我躲在床底下。

3. The gift is under the Christmas tree.
   那礼物在圣诞树下。

4. The dog is under the table.
   小狗在桌子下。

5. The monkey is under the tree.
   猴子在树下。

6. I put my bag under the chair.
   我把皮包放在椅子底下。

by　介词

1. I came here by car.
   我乘车来这里。

2. I came here by bus.
   我坐巴士来。

3. I passed by the bookshop.
   我经过那间书局。

4. I paid by my credit card.
   我用我的信用卡付。

5. I walk by the river.
   我沿着河边走。

6. I stay by the sea.
   我住在海边。

countable nouns   能够数的名词

1. I have a computer.
   我有一个电脑。

2. I have a dream.
   我有一个梦想。

3. I have a secret.
   我有一个秘密。

4. I have a mango.
   我有一个芒果。

5. I have a basket.
   我有一个篮子。

6. I have a vacuum cleaner.
   我有一台吸尘机。

1. I have a few computers.
   我有几架电脑。

2. I have a few bags.
   我有几个皮包。

3. I have a few dustbins.
   我有几个垃圾桶。

4. I have a few mangoes.
   我有几个芒果。

5. I have a few baskets.
   我有几个篮子。

6. I have a few colleagues.
   我有几个同事。

1. I have some chairs.
   我有一些椅子。

2. I have some books.
   我有一些书本。

3. I have some magazines.
   我有一些杂志。

4. I have some socks.
   我有一些袜子。

5. I have some oranges.
   我有一些橙子。

6. I have some cucumbers.
   我有一些黄瓜。

1. I have many pencils.
   我有很多铅笔。

2. I have many children.
   我有很多孩子。

3. I have many fans.
   我有很多风扇。

4. I have many tomatoes.
   我有很多番茄。

5. I have many plates.
   我有很多盘子。

6. I have many friends.
   我有很多朋友。

1. I have a lot of spoons.
   我有很多汤匙。

2. I have a lot of problems.
   我有很多问题。

3. I have a lot of oranges.
   我有很多橙子。

4. I have a lot of eggs.
   我有很多鸡蛋。

5. I have a lot of story books.
   我有很多故事书。

6. I have a lot of flowers.
   我有很多花。

uncountable nouns 不能够数的名词

1. I have a little sugar.
   我有一点点糖。

2. I have a little salt.
   我有一点点盐。

3. I have a little honey.
   我有一点点蜜糖。

4. I have a little sauce.
   我有一点点酱料。

5. I have a little flour.
   我有一点点面粉。

6. I have a little apple juice.
   我有一点点苹果汁。

1. I have some coffee powder.
   我有一些咖啡粉。

2. I have some money.
   我有一些钱。

3. I have some chilli sauce.
   我有一些辣椒酱。

4. I have some fruit juice.
   我有一些果汁。

5. I have some salad sauce.
   我有一些沙拉酱。

6. I have some ketchup.
   我有一些番茄酱。

1. I have a lot of salt.
   我有很多盐。

2. I have a lot of flour.
   我有很多面粉。

3. I have a lot of soup.
   我有很多汤。

4. I have a lot of money.
   我有很多钱。

5. I have a lot of porridge.
   我有很多粥。

6. I have a lot of fruit juice.
   我有很多果汁。

there is / there are   那里有

用在能够数的名词

1. There is a table in the room.
   房间里有一张桌子。

2. There is a fan in the room.
   房间里有一个风扇。

3. There is a mirror in the room.
   房间里有一面镜子。

4. There is a bed in the room.
   房间里有一张床。

5. There is a kite in the room.
   房间里有一个风筝。

6. There is a desk in the room.
   房间里有一张书桌。

1. There are some chairs in the room.
   房间里有一些椅子。

2. There are two fans in the room.
   房间里有两个风扇。

3. There are a few mirrors in the room.
   房间里有几面镜子。

4. There are four beds in the room.
   房间里有四张床。

5. There are some boxes in the room.
   房间里有一些箱子。

6. There are a few reporters in the
   room.
   房间里有几位记者。

1. There are many bottles in the room.
   这房间里有很多瓶子。

2. There are a lot of people in the room.
   这房间里有很多人。

3. There are many computers in the room.
   这房间里有很多电脑。

4. There are a lot of books in the room
   这房间里有很多书本。

5. There are many shoes in the room
   这房间里有很多鞋子。

6. There are a lot of magazines in the room.
   这房间里有很多杂志。

there is   那里有

用在 不能够数的名词

1. There is a little sugar in the bowl.
碗里有一点糖。

2. There is a little jam in the bowl.
碗里有一点酱料。

3. There is a little soup in the bowl.
碗里有一点汤。

4. There is a little flour in the bowl.
碗里有一点面粉。

5. There is a little salt in the bowl.
碗里有一点盐。

6. There is a little pepper in the bowl.
碗里有一点胡椒粉。

1. There is some porridge in the bowl.
   这碗里有一些粥。

2. There is some rice in the bowl.
   这碗里有一些饭。

3. There is some butter in the bowl.
   这碗里有一些牛油。

4. There is some oil in the bowl.
   这碗里有一些油。

5. There is some salt in the bowl.
   这碗里有一些盐。

6. There is some soy sauce in the bowl.
   这碗里有一些酱油。

1. There is a lot of water in the bottle.
   瓶子里有很多水。

2. There is a lot of wine in the bottle.
   瓶子里有很多酒。

3. There is a lot of oil in the bottle.
   瓶子里有很多油。

4. There is a lot of pepper in the bottle.
   瓶子里有很多胡椒粉。

5. There is a lot of orange juice in the bottle.
   瓶子里有很多橙汁。

6. There is a lot of lemon juice in the bottle.
   瓶子里有很多柠檬汁。

between 之间

1. I sat between Mary and John.
我坐在玛丽和约翰的中间。

2. I stood between Mary and John.
我站在玛丽和约翰的中间。

3. There is a tree between the two houses.
两间屋子的中间有一棵树。

4. There is a lamp between the two chairs.
两张椅子的中间有一盏灯。

5. The shop is between the two houses.
那间店是在两间屋子的中间。

3. 不同代名词的句子

have   有

1. I have a goal.
   我有一个目标。

2. You have a goal.
   你有一个目标。

3. We have a goal.
   我们有一个目标。

4. They have a goal.
   他们有一个目标。

5. He has a goal.
   他有一个目标。

6. She has a goal.
   她有一个目标。

like　喜欢

1. I like the balcony.
   我喜欢那个阳台。

2. You like the balcony.
   你喜欢那个阳台。

3. We like the balcony.
   我们喜欢那个阳台。

4. They like the balcony.
   他们喜欢那个阳台。

5. He likes the balcony.
   他喜欢那个阳台。

6. She likes the balcony.
   她喜欢那个阳台。

me 我

1. He encouraged me.
   他鼓励我。

2. He encouraged you.
   他鼓励你。

3. He encouraged us.
   他鼓励我们。

4. He encouraged them.
   他鼓励他们。

5. I encouraged him.
   我鼓励他。

6. I encouraged her.
   我鼓励她。

1. He helped me.
   他帮我。

2. He helped you.
   他帮你。

3. He helped us.
   他帮我们。

4. He helped them.
   他帮他们。

5. I helped him.
   我帮他。

6. I helped her.
   我帮她。

my   我的

1. My boss is kind.
   我的老板很善良。

2. Your boss is kind.
   你的老板很善良。

3. Our boss is kind.
   我们的老板很善良。

4. Their boss is kind.
   他们的老板很善良。

5. His boss is kind.
   他的老板很善良。

6. Her boss is kind.
   她的老板很善良。

1. My bicycle is expensive.
   我的自行车很贵。

2. Your bicycle is expensive.
   你的自行车很贵。

3. Our bicycle is expensive.
   我们的自行车很贵。

4. Their bicycle is expensive.
   他们的自行车很贵。

5. His bicycle is expensive.
   他的自行车很贵。

6. Her bicycle is expensive.
   她的自行车很贵。

present tense 现在式

1. I go to work everyday.
   我每天去上班。

2. You go to work everyday.
   你每天去上班。

3. We go to work everyday.
   我们每天去上班。

4. They go to work everyday.
   他们每天去上班。

5. He goes to work everyday.
   他每天去上班。

6. She goes to work everyday.
   她每天去上班。

present continuous tense   现在进行式

1. I am watching a movie now.
   我现在在看电影。

2. You are watching a movie now.
   你现在在看电影。

3. We are watching a movie now.
   我们现在在看电影。

4. They are watching a movie now.
   他们现在在看电影。

5. He is watching a movie now.
   他现在在看电影。

6. She is watching a movie now.
   她现在在看电影。

present perfect tense　现在完成式

1. I have mailed the letter.
   我已经寄了这封信。

2. You have mailed the letter.
   你已经寄了这封信。

3. We have mailed the letter.
   我们已经寄了这封信。

4. They have mailed the letter.
   他们已经寄了这封信。

5. He has mailed the letter.
   他已经寄了这封信。

6. She has mailed the letter.
   她已经寄了这封信。

past tense　过去式

1. I wrote a letter yesterday.
   昨天我写了一封信。

2. You wrote a letter yesterday.
   昨天你写了一封信。

3. We wrote a letter yesterday.
   昨天我们写了一封信。

4. They wrote a letter yesterday.
   昨天他们写了一封信。

5. He wrote a letter yesterday.
   昨天他写了一封信。

6. She wrote a letter yesterday.
   昨天她写了一封信。

past continuous tense　过去进行式

1. I was sweeping the floor just now.
   我刚才在扫地。

2. You were sweeping the floor just now.
   你刚才在扫地。

3. We were sweeping the floor just now.
   我们刚才在扫地。

4. They were sweeping the floor just now.
   他们刚才在扫地。

5. She was sweeping the floor just now.
   她刚才在扫地。

future tense　未来式

1. I shall clean the toilet tomorrow.
明天我将洗厕所。

2. You will clean the toilet tomorrow.
明天你将洗厕所。

3. We shall clean the toilet tomorrow.
明天我们将洗厕所。

4. They will clean the toilet tomorrow.
明天他们将洗厕所。

5. He will clean the toilet tomorrow.
明天他将洗厕所。

6. She will clean the toilet tomorrow.
明天她将洗厕所。

am 是 - 现在式

1. I am a nurse.
   我是一名护士。

2. You are a nurse.
   你是一名护士。

3. We are nurses.
   我们是护士。

4. They are nurses.
   他们是护士。

5. She is a nurse.
   她是一名护士。

6. He is a nurse.
   他是一名护士。

1. I am healthy.
   我很健康。

2. You are healthy.
   你很健康。

3. We are healthy.
   我们很健康。

4. They are healthy.
   他们很健康。

5. He is healthy.
   他很健康。

6. She is healthy.
   她很健康。

have been 是 － 现在完成式

1. I have been a doctor for three years.
我当医生已有三年了。

2. You have been a doctor for three years.
你当医生已有三年了。

3. We have been doctors for three years.
我们当医生已有三年了。

4. They have been doctors for three years.
他们当医生已有三年了。

5. He has been a doctor for three years.
他当医生已有三年了。

1. I have been busy.
   我一直很忙。

2. You have been busy.
   你一直很忙。

3. We have been busy.
   我们一直很忙。

4. They have been busy.
   他们一直很忙。

5. He has been busy.
   他一直很忙。

6. She has been busy.
   她一直很忙。

was   是 - 过去式

1. I was a singer in the past.
   我以前是一名歌手。

2. You were a singer in the past.
   你以前是一名歌手。

3. We were singers in the past.
   我们以前是歌手。

4. They were singers in the past.
   他们以前是歌手。

5. He was a singer in the past.
   他以前是一名歌手。

6. She was a singer in the past.
   她以前是一名歌手。

1. I was angry just now.
刚才我很生气。

2. You were angry just now.
刚才你很生气。

3. We were angry just now.
刚才我们很生气。

4. They were angry just now.
刚才他们很生气。

5. He was angry just now.
刚才他很生气。

6. She was angry just now.
刚才她很生气。

had been　是 – 过去完成式

1. I had been a businessman before I went to America.
我去美国前，一直是一名商人。

2. You had been a businessman before you went to America.
你去美国前，一直是一名商人。

3. We had been businessmen before we went to America.
我们去美国前，一直是商人。

4. They had been businessmen before they went to America.
他们去美国前，一直是商人。

5. He had been a businessman before he went to America.
他去美国前，一直是一名商人。

1. I had been rich before I got married.
   我结婚之前，一直很富有。

2. You had been rich before you got married.
   你结婚之前，一直很富有。

3. We had been rich before we got married.
   我们结婚之前，一直很富有。

4. They had been rich before they got married.
   他们结婚之前，一直很富有。

5. He had been rich before he got married.
   他结婚之前，一直很富有。

6. She had been rich before she got married.
   她结婚之前，一直很富有。

will be　是 － 未来式

1. I shall be a singer.
   我将成为一名歌手。

2. You will be a singer.
   你将成为一名歌手。

3. We shall be singers.
   我们将成为歌手。

4. They will be singers.
   他们将成为歌手。

5. He will be a singer.
   他将成为一名歌手。

6. She will be a singer.
   她将成为一名歌手。

1. I shall be hardworking.
   我将会很勤劳。

2. You will be hardworking.
   你将会很勤劳。

3. We shall be hardworking.
   我们将会很勤劳。

4. They will be hardworking.
   他们将会很勤劳。

5. He will be hardworking.
   他将会很勤劳。

6. She will be hardworking.
   她将会很勤劳。

4. 否定句子

like 喜欢

1. I do not like the actor.
   我不喜欢这位男演员。

2. I do not like the song.
   我不喜欢这首歌。

3. I do not like the house.
   我不喜欢这间屋子。

4. I do not like the idea.
   我不喜欢这个主意。

5. I do not like the picture.
   我不喜欢这幅画。

6. I do not like the singer.
   我不喜欢这位歌星。

can 会 / 可以

1. I can't drive.
   我不会驾车。

2. I can't sing.
   我不会唱歌。

3. I can't make cakes.
   我不会做蛋糕。

4. I can't play violin.
   我不会拉小提琴。

5. I can't play piano.
   我不会弹钢琴。

6. I can't play guitar.
   我不会弹吉他。

this   这个

1. This is not a lie.
   这不是一个谎言。

2. This is not a clock.
   这不是一个时钟。

3. This is not a hotel.
   这不是一间酒店。

4. This is not a pot.
   这不是一个锅。

5. This is not a flag.
   这不是一幅国旗。

6. This is not a dream.
   这不是一个梦。

these   这些

1. These are not birds.
   这些不是鸟。

2. These are not curtains.
   这些不是窗帘。

3. These are not stools.
   这些不是凳子。

4. These are not cucumbers.
   这些不是黄瓜。

5. These are not jokes.
   这些不是笑话。

6. These are not toys.
   这些不是玩具。

that   那个

1. That is not a monkey.
那不是一只猴子。

2. That is not a suitcase.
那不是一个手提箱。

3. That is not a kangaroo.
那不是一只袋鼠。

4. That is not a helicopter.
那不是一架直升机。

5. That is not a ship.
那不是一艘船。

6. That is not a dustbin.
那不是一个垃圾桶。

those 那些

1. Those are not onions.
   那些不是洋葱。

2. Those are not dictionaries.
   那些不是字典。

3. Those are not tidbits.
   那些不是零食。

4. Those are not fruits.
   那些不是水果。

5. Those are not insects.
   那些不是昆虫。

6. Those are not butterflies.
   那些不是蝴蝶。

have　有

1. I do not have a plan.
我没有一个计划。

2. I do not have any plans.
我没有任何计划。

3. I do not have a few plans.
我没有几个计划。

4. I do not have many plans.
我没有很多计划。

5. I do not have a lot of plans.
我没有很多计划。

6. I do not have a lot of opinions.
我没有很多意见。

1. I do not have any sugar.
   我没有糖。

2. I do not have any flour.
   我没有面粉。

3. I do not have any fruit juice.
   我没有果汁。

4. I do not have any honey.
   我没有蜜糖。

5. I do not have a lot of money.
   我没有很多钱。

6. I do not have a lot of rice.
   我没有很多米。

verb tenses 动词的时式

1. I do not watch television everyday.
   我没有每天看电视。

2. I am not watching television now.
   我现在没有在看电视。

3. I have not watched television.
   我还没有看电视。

4. I did not watch television yesterday.
   昨天我没有看电视。

5. I was not watching television this morning.
   我早上没有在看电视。

6. I shall not watch television tomorrow.
   明天我将不会看电视。

am 是

1. I am not a chef.
   我不是一名厨师。

2. I have not been a chef for 5 years.
   我不当厨师已有五年了。

3. I was not a chef in the past.
   我以前不是一名厨师。

4. I had not been a chef before I went
   to Singapore.
   我去新加坡前，没有当过厨师。

5. I shall not be a chef.
   我将不会当厨师。

6. I shall not be a police.
   我将不会当警察。

1. I am not happy.
   我不开心。

2. I have not been happy.
   我一直不开心。

3. I was not happy yesterday.
   昨天我不开心。

4. I had not been happy before I got married.
   我结婚前，一直不开心。

5. I shall not be happy.
   我将会不开心。

6. I shall not be afraid.
   我将不会害怕。

there are no 那里没有

用在能够数的名词

1. There are no mangoes in the basket.
这篮子里没有芒果。

2. There are no watermelons in the basket.
这篮子里没有西瓜。

3. There are no pears in the basket.
这篮子里没有梨。

4. There are no coconuts in the basket.
这篮子里没有椰子。

5. There are no durians in the basket.
这篮子里没有榴莲。

6. There are no balls in the basket.
这篮子里没有球。

there is no   那里没有

用在不能够数的名词

1. There is no water in the bottle.
   这瓶子里没有水。

2. There is no milk in the bottle.
   这瓶子里没有牛奶。

3. There is no lemon juice in the bottle.
   这瓶子里没有柠檬汁。

4. There is no coffee in the bottle.
   这瓶子里没有咖啡。

5. There is no tea in the bottle.
   这瓶子里没有茶。

6. There is no chilli sauce in the bottle.
   这瓶子里没有辣椒酱。

5. 简单的问题

who 谁

1. Who can write?
   谁会写?

2. Who can drive?
   谁会驾车?

3. Who can sing?
   谁会唱歌?

4. Who can play badminton?
   谁会打羽毛球?

5. Who can cook curry chicken?
   谁会煮咖喱鸡?

6. Who can ride bicycle?
   谁会骑自行车?

1. Who wants to explain?
   谁要解释?

2. Who wants to guess?
   谁要猜?

3. Who wants to try?
   谁要试试?

4. Who wants to do?
   谁要做?

5. Who wants to borrow?
   谁要借?

6. Who wants to sell?
   谁要卖?

1. Who wants to play basketball?
   谁要打篮球？

2. Who wants to call him?
   谁要打电话给他？

3. Who wants to go for lunch?
   谁要去吃午餐？

4. Who wants to book the hotel?
   谁要订饭店？

5. Who wants to do housework?
   谁要做家务？

6. Who wants to earn money?
   谁要赚钱？

1. Who wants to go to the zoo?
   谁要去动物园?

2. Who wants to go to the supermarket?
   谁要去超级市场?

3. Who wants to go to the post office?
   谁要去邮政局?

4. Who wants to go to the canteen?
   谁要去食堂?

5. Who wants to go to the club?
   谁要去俱乐部?

6. Who wants to go to the museum?
   谁要去博物馆?

1. Who are you?
   你是谁?

2. Who are they
   他们是谁?

3. Who is he?
   他是谁?

4. Who is she?
   她是谁?

5. Who is the boss?
   谁是老板?

6. Who is the manager?
   谁是经理?

1. Who helps the teacher everyday?
   谁每天帮老师?

2. Who is helping the teacher now?
   谁正在帮老师?

3. Who has helped the teacher?
   谁已经帮了老师?

4. Who helped the teacher yesterday?
   谁昨天帮了老师?

5. Who was helping the teacher just now?
   刚才谁正在帮老师?

6. Who will help the teacher tomorrow?
   明天谁会帮老师?

1. Who is a lawyer?
   谁是一名律师?

2. Who has been a lawyer for 3 years?
   谁当律师已有三年了?

3. Who was a lawyer in the past?
   谁以前是一名律师?

4. Who had been a lawyer before he went to France?
   谁去法国前, 一直是一名律师?

5. Who will be a lawyer?
   谁将会成为一名律师?

6. Who will be a hairdresser?
   谁将会成为一名美发师?

1. Who is hardworking?
   谁很勤劳?

2. Who have been hardworking?
   谁一直很勤劳?

3. Who was hardworking yesterday?
   谁昨天很勤劳?

4. Who had been hardworking before
   he got married?
   谁结婚前一直很勤劳?

5. Who will be hardworking?
   谁将会很勤劳?

6. Who will be free tomorrow?
   谁明天有空?

where 哪里

1. Where is the toilet?
   厕所在哪里?

2. Where is the post office?
   邮政局在哪里?

3. Where is the car park?
   停车场在哪里?

4. Where is the hotel?
   饭店在哪里?

5. Where is the shopping centre?
   购物中心在哪里?

6. Where is the café?
   咖啡馆在哪里?

1. Where are my books?
   我的书本在哪里?

2. Where are the students?
   学生们在哪里?

3. Where are the balloons?
   气球在哪里?

4. Where are the magazines?
   杂志在哪里?

5. Where are the shoes?
   鞋子在哪里?

6. Where are my parents?
   我的父母在哪里?

1. Where do you go everyday?
你每天去哪里?

2. Where are you going now?
你现在去哪里?

3. Where have you gone?
你去哪里了?

4. Where did you go yesterday?
昨天你去了哪里?

5. Where were you going just now?
刚才你正要去哪里?

6. Where will you go tomorrow?
明天你将要去哪里?

1. Where does he go everyday?
   他每天去哪里?

2. Where is he going now?
   他现在去哪里?

3. Where has he gone?
   他 去哪里了?

4. Where did he go yesterday?
   昨天他去了哪里?

5. Where was he going just now?
   刚才他正要去哪里?

6. Where will he go tomorrow?
   明天他将会去哪里?

what 什么

1. What is your name?
   你叫什么名?

2. What is your goal?
   你的目标是什么?

3. What is your dream?
   你的梦想是什么?

4. What is your hobby?
   你的爱好是什么?

5. What is your favourite food?
   你最喜欢吃什么食物?

6. What is your plan?
   你有什么计划?

1. What can you cook?
   你会煮什么?

2. What can you write?
   你会写什么?

3. What can you teach?
   你会教什么?

4. What can he cook?
   他会煮什么?

5. What can he write?
   他会写什么?

6. What can he teach?
   他会教什么?

1. What do you like to repair?
你喜欢修理什么?

2. What do you like to wash?
你喜欢洗什么?

3. What do like to plant?
你喜欢种什么?

4. What does he like to repair?
他喜欢修理什么?

5. What does he like to wash?
他喜欢洗什么?

6. What does he like to plant?
他喜欢种什么?

1. What do you want to find?
   你要找什么?

2. What do you want to say?
   你要讲什么?

3. What do you want to discuss?
   你要讨论什么?

4. What does he want to find?
   他要找什么?

5. What does he want to say?
   他要讲什么?

6. What does he want to discuss?
   他要讨论什么?

1. What is this?
   这是什么?

2. What is that?
   那是什么?

3. What are these?
   这些是什么?

4. What are those?
   那些是什么?

5. What is in the bag?
   皮包里有什么?

6. What are the choices?
   选择有哪些?

1. What do you learn everyday?
   你每天学什么?

2. What are you learning now?
   你现在在学什么?

3. What have you learnt?
   你学了什么?

4. What did you learn yesterday?
   昨天你学什么?

5. What were you learning just now?
   刚才你在学什么?

6. What will you learn tomorrow?
   明天你将学什么?

1. What does he learn everyday?
   他每天学什么?

2. What is he learning now?
   他现在在学什么?

3. What has he learnt?
   他学了什么?

4. What did he learn yesterday?
   昨天他学什么?

5. What was he learning just now?
   刚才他在学什么?

6. What will he learn tomorrow?
   明天他将学什么?

why　为什么

1. Why do you cry everyday?
为什么你每天哭?

2. Why are you crying now?
为什么你在哭?

3. Why have you cried?
为什么你哭了?

4. Why did you cry yesterday?
为什么你昨天哭?

5. Why were you crying just now?
为什么你刚才在哭?

6. Why were you laughing just now?
为什么你刚才在笑?

1. Why does he cry everyday?
为什么他每天哭?

2. Why is he crying now?
为什么他在哭?

3. Why has he cried?
为什么他哭了?

4. Why did he cry yesterday?
为什么他昨天哭?

5. Why was he crying just now?
为什么他刚才在哭?

6. Why was he laughing just now?
为什么他刚才在笑?

1. Why are you sad?
   为什么你很伤心?

2. Why have you been sad?
   为什么你一直很伤心?

3. Why were you sad yesterday?
   为什么你昨天很伤心?

4. Why had you been sad before you got married?
   为什么你结婚前一直很伤心?

5. Why will you be sad?
   为什么你将会很伤心?

6. Why will you be disappointed?
   为什么你将会很失望?

1. Why is he sad?
   为什么他很伤心?

2. Why has he been sad
   为什么他一直很伤心?

3. Why was he sad yesterday?
   为什么他昨天很伤心?

4. Why had he been sad before he got married?
   为什么他结婚前一直很伤心?

5. Why will he be sad?
   为什么他将会很伤心?

6. Why will he be disappointed?
   为什么他将会很失望?

which 哪一个

1. Which game do you play everyday?
   你每天玩哪一个游戏?

2. Which game are you playing now?
   你现在在玩哪一个游戏?

3. Which game have you played?
   你已经玩了哪一个游戏?

4. Which game did you play yesterday?
   你昨天玩哪一个游戏?

5. Which game were you playing just now?
   你刚才在玩哪一个游戏?

6. Which game will you play tomorrow?
   你明天将玩哪一个游戏?

1. Which game does he play everyday?
   他每天玩哪一个游戏？

2. Which game is he playing now?
   他现在在玩哪一个游戏？

3. Which game has he played?
   他已经玩了哪一个游戏？

4. Which game did he play yesterday?
   他昨天玩哪一个游戏？

5. Which game was he playing just now?
   他刚才在玩哪一个游戏？

6. Which game will he play tomorrow?
   他明天将玩哪一个游戏？

when 几时

1. When did you tell the story?
你几时讲了这个故事?

2. When did you buy the house?
你几时买了这间屋子?

3. When did you take the medicine?
你几时吃了药?

4. When did he tell the story?
他几时讲了这个故事?

5. When did he buy the house?
他几时买了这间屋子?

6. When did he take the medicine?
他几时吃了药?

1. When will you sell your car?
   你几时将会卖你的车子？

2. When will you meet your principal?
   你几时将会见你的校长？

3. When will you book the hotel?
   你几时将会定饭店？

4. When will he sell his car?
   他几时将会卖他的车子？

5. When will he meet his principal?
   他几时将会见他的校长？

6. When will he book the hotel?
   他几时将会定饭店？

whose 谁的

1. Whose bed is this?
   这是谁的床?

2. Whose jacket is this?
   这是谁的外套?

3. Whose child is this?
   这是谁的孩子?

4. Whose passport is this?
   这是谁的护照?

5. Whose wallet is this?
   这是谁的钱包?

6. Whose mobile phone is this?
   这是谁的手机?

1. Whose toys are these?
   这些是谁的玩具？

2. Whose clothes are these?
   这些是谁的衣服？

3. Whose pets are these?
   这些是谁的宠物？

4. Whose keys are these?
   这些是谁的钥匙？

5. Whose ideas are these?
   这些是谁的主意？

6. Whose pants are these?
   这些是谁的长裤？

do   问词

1. Do you like the gift?
   你喜欢这个礼物吗?

2. Do you like the flower vase?
   你喜欢这个花瓶吗?

3. Do you like the comb?
   你喜欢这支梳子吗?

4. Does he like the gift?
   他喜欢这个礼物吗?

5. Does he like the flower vase?
   他喜欢这个花瓶吗?

6. Does he like the comb?
   他喜欢这支梳子吗?

1. Do you like to exercise?
   你喜欢运动吗?

2. Do you like to work?
   你喜欢工作吗?

3. Do you like to travel?
   你喜欢旅行吗?

4. Does he like to exercise?
   他喜欢运动吗?

5. Does he like to work?
   他喜欢工作吗?

6. Does he like to travel?
   他喜欢旅行吗?

1. Do you like to take bus?
   你喜欢搭巴士吗？

2. Do you like to iron clothes?
   你喜欢烫衣服吗？

3. Do you like to teach children?
   你喜欢教小孩子吗？

4. Does he like to take bus?
   他喜欢搭巴士吗？

5. Does he like to iron clothes?
   他喜欢烫衣服吗？

6. Does he like to teach children?
   他喜欢教小孩子吗？

1. Do you want to see?
   你要看吗?

2. Do you want to jump?
   你要跳吗?

3. Do you want to guess?
   你要猜吗?

4. Does he want to see?
   他要看吗?

5. Does he want to jump?
   他要跳吗?

6. Does he want to guess?
   他要猜吗?

1. Do you want to play golf?
   你要打高尔夫球吗?

2. Do you want to buy a jacket?
   你要买一件外套吗?

3. Do you want to write a report?
   你要写一份报告吗?

4. Does he want to play golf?
   他要打高尔夫球吗?

5. Does he want to buy a jacket?
   他要买一件外套吗?

6. Does he want to write a report?
   他要写一份报告吗?

1. Do you want to go to the museum?
   你要去博物院吗？

2. Do you want to go to the playground?
   你要去游乐场吗？

3. Do you want to go to the canteen?
   你要去食堂吗？

4. Does he want to go to the museum?
   他要去博物院吗？

5. Does he want to go to the playground?
   他要去游乐场吗？

6. Does he want to go to the canteen?
   他要去食堂吗？

1. Do you have a washing machine?
   你有一台洗衣机吗?

2. Do you have any chairs?
   你有椅子吗?

3. Do you have any money?
   你有钱吗?

4. Does he have a washing machine?
   他有一台洗衣机吗?

5. Does he have any chairs?
   他有椅子吗?

6. Does he have any money?
   他有钱吗?

1. Do you watch television everyday?
   你有没有每天看电视?

2. Are you watching television now?
   你现在是不是在看电视?

3. Have you watched television?
   你看电视了吗?

4. Did you watch television yesterday?
   你昨天有看电视吗?

5. Were you watching television just now?
   你刚才是不是在看电视?

6. Will you watch television tomorrow?
   你明天会看电视吗?

1. Does he watch television everyday?
   他有没有每天看电视?

2. Is he watching television now?
   他现在是不是在看电视?

3. Has he watched television?
   他已经看电视了吗?

4. Did he watch television yesterday?
   他昨天有看电视吗?

5. Was he watching television just now?
   他刚才在看电视是吗?

6. Will he watch television tomorrow?
   他明天将会看电视吗?

are 是

1. Are you a model?
   你是模特儿吗?

2. Have you been a model for 5 years?
   你当模特儿有五年了吗?

3. Were you a model in the past?
   你以前是一名模特儿吗?

4. Had you been a model before you went to Hong Kong?
   你去香港前, 一直当模特儿吗?

5. Will you be a model?
   你将会当模特儿吗?

6. Will you be an engineer?
   你将会当工程师吗?

1. Is he a model?
   他是模特儿吗?

2. Has he been a model for 5 years?
   他当模特儿有五年了吗?

3. Was he a model in the past?
   他以前是一名模特儿吗?

4. Had he been a model before he went to Hong Kong?
   他去香港前, 一直当模特儿吗?

5. Will he be a model?
   他将会当模特儿吗?

6. Will he be an engineer?
   他将会当工程师吗?

1. Are u popular?
   你受欢迎吗？

2. Have you been popular?
   你一直以来都受欢迎吗？

3. Were you popular in the past?
   你以前受欢迎吗？

4. Had you been popular before you got married?
   你结婚之前，一直受欢迎吗？

5. Will you be popular?
   你将会受欢迎吗？

6. Will you be disappointed?
   你将会失望吗？

1. Is he popular?
   他受欢迎吗?

2. Has he been popular?
   他一直受欢迎吗?

3. Was he popular in the past?
   他以前受欢迎吗?

4. Had he been popular before he got married?
   他结婚之前, 一直受欢迎吗?

5. Will he be popular?
   他将会受欢迎吗?

6. Will he be disappointed?
   他将会失望吗?

how many   几个

用在能够数的名词

1. How many siblings do you have?
   你有几个兄弟姐妹？

2. How many candles do you have?
   你有几根蜡烛？

3. How many pears do you have?
   你有几个梨子？

4. How many siblings does he have?
   他有几个兄弟姐妹？

5. How many candles does he have?
   他有几根蜡烛？

6. How many pears does he have?
   他有几个梨子？

1. How many eggs do you buy everyday?
   你每天买几个鸡蛋?

2. How many eggs are you buying now?
   你现在要买几个鸡蛋?

3. How many eggs have you bought?
   你已经买了几个鸡蛋?

4. How many eggs did you buy yesterday?
   你昨天买了几个鸡蛋?

5. How many eggs were you buying just now?
   你刚才在买几个鸡蛋?

6. How many eggs will you buy tomorrow?
   你明天将买几个鸡蛋?

1. How many eggs does he buy everyday?
他每天买几个鸡蛋?

2. How many eggs is he buying now?
他现在要买几个鸡蛋?

3. How many eggs has he bought?
他已经买了几个鸡蛋?

4. How many eggs did he buy yesterday?
他昨天买了几个鸡蛋?

5. How many eggs was he buying just now?
他刚才在买几个鸡蛋?

6. How many eggs will he buy tomorrow?
他明天将买几个鸡蛋?

how much　多少

用在不能够数的名词

1. How much money do you have?
你有多少钱?

2. How much flour do you have?
你有多少面粉?

3. How much oil do you have?
你有多少油?

4. How much money does he have?
他有多少钱?

5. How much flour does he have?
他有多少面粉?

6. How much oil does he have?
他有多少油?

1. How much flour do you put?
   你放多少面粉？

2. How much flour are you putting now?
   你现在放多少面粉？

3. How much flour have you put?
   你已经放了多少面粉？

4. How much flour did you put yesterday?
   昨天你放了多少面粉？

5. How much flour were you putting just now?
   刚才你正在放多少面粉？

6. How much flour will you put tomorrow?
   明天你将会放多少面粉？

1. How much flour does he put?
   他放多少面粉?

2. How much flour is he putting now?
   他现在放多少面粉?

3. How much flour has he put?
   他已经放了多少面粉?

4. How much flour did he put yesterday?
   昨天他放了多少面粉?

5. How much flour was he putting just now?
   刚才他正在放多少面粉?

6. How much flour will he put tomorrow?
   明天他将会放多少面粉?

how   怎样

1. How to play?
   怎样玩?

2. How to sew?
   怎样缝?

3. How to do?
   怎样做?

4. How to imagine?
   怎样想像?

5. How to repair?
   怎样修理?

6. How to explain?
   怎样解释?

1. How to solve this problem?
   怎样解决这个问题?

2. How to cook beef?
   怎样煮牛肉?

3. How to arrange flowers?
   怎样插花?

4. How to save money?
   怎样省钱?

5. How to make money?
   怎样赚钱?

6. How to make kites?
   怎样制作风筝?

1. How to go to the airport?
   怎样去机场?

2. How to go to the supermarket?
   怎样去超级市场?

3. How to go to the library?
   怎样去图书馆?

4. How to go to the beach?
   怎样去海边?

5. How to go to the railway station?
   怎样去火车站?

6. How to go to the clinic?
   怎样去诊所?

1. How to be a magician?
   怎样成为魔术师?

2. How to be a writer?
   怎样成为作家?

3. How to be a manager?
   怎样成为经理?

4. How to be a chef?
   怎样成为厨师?

5. How to be an engineer?
   怎样成为工程师?

6. How to be a nurse?
   怎样成为护士?

1. How to be happy?
   怎样才能快乐?

2. How to be healthy?
   怎样保持身体健康?

3. How to be famous?
   怎样才能出名?

4. How to be slim?
   怎样变得苗条?

5. How to be successful?
   怎样才会成功?

6. How to be smart?
   怎样变得聪明?

1. How do you draw lions?
   你怎样画狮子？

2. How do you answer this question?
   你怎样回答这问题？

3. How do you order the food?
   你怎样点菜？

4. How does he draw lions?
   他怎样画狮子？

5. How does he answer this question?他
   怎样回答这问题？

6. How does he order the food?
   他怎样点菜？

1. How did you cook spaghetti?
   你怎样煮意大利面?

2. How did you solve the problem?
   你怎样解决了这问题?

3. How did you find your wallet?
   你怎样找到了你的钱包?

4. How did he cook spaghetti?
   他怎样煮意大利面?

5. How did he solve the problem?
   他怎样解决了这问题

6. How did he find his wallet?
   他怎样找到了他的钱包?

can 会 / 可以

1. Can you speak English?
   你会讲英语吗?

2. Can you swim?
   你会游泳吗?

3. Can you drive?
   你会驾车吗?

4. Can he speak English?
   他会讲英语吗?

5. Can he swim?
   他会游泳吗?

6. Can he drive?
   他会驾车吗?

6. 常见的短语和句子

Hello
哈啰

Goodbye
再见

I am fine.
我很好。

Nice to meet you
很高兴认识你

Thank you
谢谢

Cheers
干杯

You are welcome.
不客气

Very funny
很好笑

Welcome
不客气

Wish you well!
祝你一切都好!

See you
再见

Well done
做得好

Good morning
早安

So delicious
真美味

Good afternoon
午安

Get well soon!
祝你早日康复!

Good evening
傍晚好

Excuse me
请让一让

Good night
晚安

I am sorry.
真对不起

I beg your pardon.
请再说一遍。

Wish you good luck!
祝你好运。

Sorry I am late.
对不起，我迟到了。

Please come in
请进

I will be late.
我将会迟些。

Bill please
买单

Please take a seat.
请坐

Please hold on
请等一下

Please forgive me.
请原谅我

Don't worry
不用担心

Congratulations
恭喜

It's simply perfect!
这真是完美!

Oh my God!
我的天啊!

It's incredible.
真是难以相信。

What a coincidence
真凑巧!

It's wonderful!
真美妙

It's a lovely day.
这是美好的一天。

I got it.
我明白了。

Have a nice trip.
祝你旅途愉快。

Too salty
太咸

Too sweet
太甜

Happy new year!
新年快乐!

Merry Christmas!
圣诞节快乐!

Happy Birthday!
生日快乐!

I love you.
我爱你。

I miss you.
我想你。

I am here.
我在这里。

I know that.
我知道

I am fine, thank you.
我很好, 谢谢。

My name is John.
我的名字是约翰。

I am Susan.
我是苏珊。

You look good.
你看起来挺好的。

I am from Singapore.
我来自新加坡。

Today is Monday.
今天是星期一。

Tomorrow is Tuesday.
明天是星期二。

I am going for a holiday.
我要去度假。

7. 常见的问题

How are you?
你好吗?

Who are you?
你是谁?

What is your height?
你身高多少?

How is everything?
一切好吗?

How's life?
近来好吗?

How old are you?
你今年几岁?

When is your birthday?
你的生日是几时?

Are you ok?
你还好吗?

Where are they?
他们在哪里?

May I know your name?
你叫什么名?

Where do you stay?
你住在哪里?
Where are you going?
你要去哪里?

Where is your office?
你的办公室在哪里?

Is this very spicy?
这道菜会辣吗?

Have you taken your dinner?
你吃晚餐了吗?

Are you done?
你好了吗?

Does it hurt?
会痛吗?

What is the time now?
现在几点?

What time are you going?
你几点要去?

How much is it?
多少钱?

May I help you?
需要我帮忙吗?

Is it cold today?
今天天气冷吗?

Shall we bring an umbrella?
我们需要带把伞吗?

How's the weather?
天气怎样?

Have you bought the air tickets?
你买机票了吗?

Have you booked the hotel?
你定饭店了吗?

8. 词汇

Number 数目

one	一
two	二
three	三
four	四
five	五
six	六
seven	七
eight	八
nine	九
ten	十
eleven	十一
twelve	十二
thirteen	十三
fourteen	十四
fifteen	十五
sixteen	十六
seventeen	十七
eighteen	十八
nineteen	十九

Beverage　饮料

tea	茶
water	水
orange juice	橙汁
fruit juice	果汁
coffee	咖啡
milk	牛奶
soft drinks	汽水
soy milk	豆花水
hot beverage	热饮
cold beverage	冷饮
beer	啤酒
mineral water	矿泉水
wine	葡萄酒
alcohol drink	酒
green tea	绿茶
lemon tea	柠檬茶
milk tea	奶茶
red wine	红酒
Jasmine tea	茉莉茶

Places　地方

restaurant	餐馆
park	公园
church	教堂
cinema	戏院
hospital	医院
playground	游乐场
library	图书馆
concert hall	音乐厅
museum	博物院
zoo	动物园
gym	健身院
swimming pool	游泳池
botanical garden	植物园
shopping centre	购物中心
supermarket	超级市场
clinic	诊所
market	菜市场
fast food restaurant	快餐店
aquarium	水族馆

Traffic　交通

boat	船
bus	巴士
car	车
truck	货车
aeroplane	飞机
helicopter	直升机
train	火车
taxi	出租车
motorcycle	摩托车
bicycle	自行车
road	马路
driver	司机
traffic light	交通灯
zebra crossing	斑马线
sidewalk	人行道
bus stop	巴士站
subway	地铁
train station	火车站
lamp post	路灯

Travel　旅行

passport	护照
luggage	行李
airport	机场
hotel	饭店
air ticket	机票
scenery	风景
map	地图
tourist	游客
camera	相机
itinerary	行程
tourist attraction	旅游景点
money changer	货币兑换
travel insurance	旅游保险
video	录像
photograph	照片
sunglasses	太阳眼镜
hat	帽子
cruise	游轮
tour guide	导游

Country   国家

China	中国
England	英国
America	美国
Australia	澳大利亚
Switzerland	瑞士
Malaysia	马来西亚
India	印度
Japan	日本
Korea	韩国
Indonesia	印尼
Cambodia	柬埔寨
Germany	德国
France	法国
Russia	俄罗斯
Vietnam	越南
Myanmar	缅甸
Italy	意大利
Spain	西班牙
New Zealand	新西兰

Office   公司

boss	老板
secretary	秘书
colleague	同事
desk	书桌
computer	电脑
email	电邮
message	简讯
fax machine	传真机
meeting	会议
employee	员工
telephone	电话
mobile phone	手机
lift	电梯
stationery	文具
reception	接待处
paper	纸
paper clip	纸夹
pantry	茶水间
building	大厦

Nature   大自然

wind	风
river	河
cloud	云
tree	树
sun	太阳
moon	月亮
star	星星
lake	湖
mountain	山
sea	海
waterfall	瀑布
sunshine	阳光
fire	火
rain	雨
snow	雪
fog	雾
flood	水灾
air	空气
soil	泥土

Time 时间

morning	早上
afternoon	下午
night	晚上
yesterday	昨天
today	今天
tomorrow	明天
next day	隔天
one day	一天
last year	去年
this year	今年
next year	明年
three years ago	三年前
two years later	两年后
once upon a time	很久以前
long time ago	很久以前
spring	春天
summer	夏天
autumn	秋天
winter	冬天

Family　家人

Father	爸爸
mother	妈妈
elder sister	姐姐
younger sister	妹妹
uncle	舅舅/叔叔
aunty	阿姨/姑姑
cousin	表姐妹/表兄弟
grandfather	公公/爷爷
grandmother	婆婆 /奶奶

Body 身体

eye	眼睛
ear	耳朵
nose	鼻子
hair	头发
face	脸
leg	脚
hand	手
nail	手指
skin	皮肤

Animals   动物

dog	狗
cat	猫
bird	鸟
tiger	老虎
lion	狮子
horse	马
goat	羊
monkey	猴子
pig	猪
snake	蛇
dragon	龙
deer	鹿
cow	牛
rat	老鼠
rabbit	兔子
tortoise	乌龟
giraffe	长颈鹿
zebra	斑马
leopard	豹

Food　食物

egg	鸡蛋
cake	蛋糕
rice	饭
noodle	面
bread	面包
fruit	水果
vegetable	蔬菜
fish	鱼
chicken	鸡

Fruits　水果

orange	橙
apple	苹果
pear	梨
grape	葡萄
banana	香蕉
papaya	木瓜
watermelon	西瓜
peach	桃子
mango	芒果
lemon	柠檬
durian	榴莲
blueberry	蓝草莓
strawberry	红草莓
cherry	樱桃
grapefruit	葡萄柚
plum	李子
prune	梅干
pineapple	凤梨
rambutan	红毛丹

School　学校

teacher	老师
student	学生
principal	校长
white board	白板
canteen	食堂
classmate	同学
homework	功课
hall	礼堂
basketball court	篮球场

House   屋子

fan	风扇
air conditioner	冷气机
table	桌子
chair	椅子
cupboard	橱
kitchen	厨房
living room	客厅
sofa	沙发
fridge	冰箱
dining room	饭厅
bedroom	睡房
balcony	阳台
vacuum cleaner	吸尘机
washing machine	洗衣机
curtain	窗帘
light	灯
coffee table	茶几
carpet	地毯
swimming pool	游泳池

Occupation 职业

doctor	医生
lawyer	律师
businessman	商人
postman	邮差
pilot	飞行员
chef	厨师
photographer	摄影师
accountant	会计师
engineer	工程师
nurse	护士
manager	经理
teacher	老师
principal	校长
writer	作家
policeman	警察
artist	艺术家
scientist	科学家
cleaner	清洁工人
musician	音乐家

To describe a person   形容一个人

pretty	美丽
handsome	英俊
fat	胖
thin	瘦
tall	高
short	矮
happy	高兴
sad	伤心
clean	清洁
dirty	肮脏
polite	有礼貌
rude	没有礼貌
intelligent	聪明
stupid	笨
hardworking	勤劳
lazy	懒惰
brave	勇敢
timid	胆小
cheerful	开朗

To describe food   形容食物

sweet	甜
sour	酸
bitter	苦
cold	冷
hot	热
salty	咸
spicy hot	辣
fragrant	香
smelly	臭
hard	硬
soft	软
crispy	酥脆
oily	油腻
delicious	美味
bland	平淡
nutritious	有营养
sumptuous	丰盛
colourful	富有色彩
fresh	新鲜

To describe a room   形容一间房间

big	大
small	小
wide	宽
narrow	窄
untidy	不整洁
neat	整齐
clean	清洁
dirty	肮脏
hot	热
cold	冷
cool	凉
comfortable	舒服
warm	温暖
bright	亮
dark	暗
spacious	宽敞
cozy	舒适
messy	乱
stylish	时尚

To describe a place　形容一个地方

far	远
near	近
noisy	很吵
quiet	很静
crowded	拥挤
beautiful	美丽
safe	安全
dangerous	危险
grand	堂皇

Colours   颜色

red	红色
yellow	黄色
orange	橙色
green	青色
blue	蓝色
purple	紫色
white	白色
black	黑色
pink	粉红色

Shapes　形状

square	四方形
rectangle	长方形
triangle	三角形
round	圆形
oval	椭圆形
rhombus	菱形
heart-shaped	心形
octagon	八角形
hexagon	六边形

Verbs 动词

eat	吃
drink	喝
talk	讲
sing	唱
smile	微笑
laugh	笑
scold	骂
shout	喊
blow	吹
see	看
wink	眨眼
hear	听
listen	听
smell	闻
walk	走
run	跑
jump	跳
dance	跳舞
play	玩

squat	蹲
kick	踢
beat	打
catch	捉
bring	带来
use	用
take	拿
comb	梳
touch	碰
draw	画
white	写
cook	煮
buy	买
sell	卖
shake	摇
keep	收
hold	握
count	数
take	拿
carry	拿; 抱
pull	拉

push	推
sweep	扫
cry	哭
wash	洗
keep	收
enjoy	享受
hug	拥抱
learn	学
press	按

动词表

现在式	过去式	完成式	
answer	answered	answered	回答
bite	bit	bitten	咬
buy	bought	bought	买
bake	baked	baked	烘
cook	cooked	cooked	煮
cry	cried	cried	哭
count	counted	counted	数
change	changed	changed	换
eat	ate	eaten	吃
enjoy	enjoyed	enjoyed	享受
earn	earned	earned	赚
do	did	done	做
dance	danced	danced	跳舞
draw	drew	drawn	画
dream	dreamt	dreamt	梦
drink	drank	drunk	喝
fly	flew	flown	飞
forget	forgot	forgotten	忘记

hear	heard	heard	听
hide	hid	hid	躲
jump	jumped	jumped	跳
keep	kept	kept	收
kick	kicked	kicked	踢
learn	learnt	learnt	学
listen	listened	listened	听
look	looked	looked	看
lose	lost	lost	输
play	played	played	玩
push	pushed	pushed	推
pull	pulled	pulled	拉
read	read	read	读
run	ran	run	跑
see	saw	seen	看
sell	sold	sold	卖
scold	scolded	scolded	骂
sing	sang	sung	唱
sit	sat	sat	坐
sleep	slept	slept	睡
share	shared	shared	分享

steal	stole	stolen	偷
sweep	swept	swept	扫
swim	swam	swum	游泳
take	took	taken	拿
talk	talked	talked	讲
think	thought	thought	想
touch	touched	touched	碰
wait	waited	waited	等
wash	washed	washed	洗
walk	walked	walked	走
wipe	wiped	wiped	抹
write	wrote	written	写
yawn	yawned	yawned	打哈欠

CPSIA information can be obtained
at www.ICGtesting.com
Printed in the USA
LVHW111534020519
616416LV00001B/198/P